A Valley To Traverse

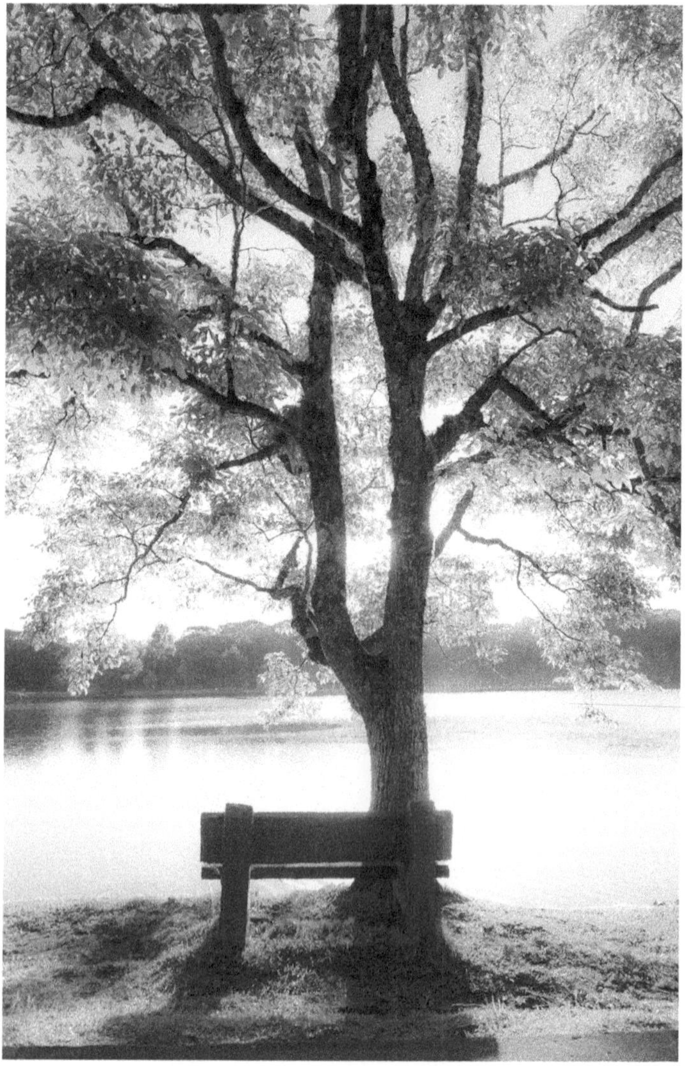

A Valley To Traverse

Poems by
Paul H Simmons

*This is the third collection of poems by
Paul Hume Simmons, following on from his previous
publications: 'A Construction in Space' (2013) and
'The Look of Beauty' (2015).*

THE CHOIR PRESS

Copyright © 2024 Paul H. Simmons

All rights reserved. No part of this publication may be reproduced or transmitted in any form or by any means, electronic or mechanical including photocopying, recording or any information storage or retrieval system, without prior permission in writing from the publishers.

The right of Paul H. Simmons to be identified as the author of this work has been asserted by him in accordance with the Copyright, Designs and Patents Act 1988

First published in the United Kingdom in 2024 by
The Choir Press

ISBN 978-1-78963-475-4

For all my family– and Michael, for all his help and encouragement

MAGENTA: Colour of universal harmony and emotional balance.

Again I raised my eyes, and this is what I saw:
four chariots coming out between two mountains,
and the mountains were mountains of bronze.

Zech. 6

But in green ruins, in the desolate walls
   Of antique palaces, where Man hath been,
Though the dun fox, or wild hyena, calls,
   And owls, that flit continually between,
Shriek to the echo, and the low winds moan,
There the true Silence is, self-conscious and alone.

from 'Silence' by Thomas Hood (1799-1845)

Contents

A valley to traverse	1
Red Lightship and the sea	2
Machines	4
The Butterfly	6
The sun in rhyme	7
A Queen enthrals	8
The ice flow	9
Commotion	10
Piecemeal	11
Vera Lucia	12
A painting in reverse	13
A village life	14
A City Life Sao Paulo style	15
Lost Copy	16
Vindication or the Worm that turned	17
Gold windows in the darkness	19
The longest village	20
A cenotaph	22
Juggernaut	23
Stern and serious	24
Identity	25
The haunting of what went before	26
Above and Below	27
American Candy	28
Salt of the earth	29
A surgeon slips away	30

Ideas, events and people	31
God speed the plough	32
Rootedness	33
Nothing like that	34
This be some other sort of verse	36
Just a thought	37
Death Doula	38
An island in the sky	39
Bright angels in decay	40
At this moment	41
A Cowboy's view	42
A Tyrant's view	43
As if there's no tomorrow	44
All in private	45
Born and bred	46
If I could write a sonnet	47
Wollemi	48
Nearly understood	49
Alma mater	50
Encounter (Candlemas)	51
Man's empty praise	52
Absurdity	53
Heedlessness	54
Reverting to type	55
Transformation	56
Solitary swansong	57

A valley to traverse

Grey skies hang in a stubborn frown,
Impossible to manipulate or break;
Penetrating suburban streets with hazy lamplight;
Drear over barren, broken fields, over brown, swollen rivers,
And seas that slowly heave to the beach, a needed embrace,
With sullen, slipping sound; extremities of place.
No reflection here, the sun is lost afar,
No twinkle or delight, and the damp, chill air
Has only the sound of remorse, no clarity to share.

But there's a bold sky with features upon the other side,
Where light becomes a colour and the scents of earth abound,
As ancient trees and saplings taste and share a common ground.
The solid mountains stand so fine; a valley to traverse,
To amble by a dimpled pool and stream as smooth as ice,
And watch while egrets sit on high, dark fish as if at play
And grasslands leaning in the breeze, with sun and mellow rain;
And biding here, and pressing there along that vacant path
We follow where the daisies grow, a place where no feet pass.

Red Lightship and the sea

The scent of the sea, the mud and then the marsh,
The hulks of boats with rope, a relic of their past;
A harbour full of bright ones shining just as new,
The proud and careful owner, intent without a crew.
The occasional and frequent, the wanderer or staid,
The voyager or tourist, all these in sun they stray;
Down past substantial moorings, a path that leads to sea,
Around the little tenders, along the estuary.
Scattered are the seabirds, pricking through the mud,
Avocets and waders with seagulls hanging up above.
The sun and cloud entrances our eyes with crazy light;
Reflection, moving water – golden to the sight.
Such clarity of view is here that strands upon the shore
Resemble sheen of sandy beach, decay in depth no more.
Above all this the Lightship parades its big red frame;
Gallant as an architect with legendary name.
And crooked narrow walkways through the slip and slide
Lead towards its prominence, stranded by the tide.

There aboard adventurers now reap their nightly stay,
While mists and murk and murmurs attend the close of day.
Then way out in the dark sea, past all created crafts,
Past all the empty vessels and skeletons of masts,
The salt and sounds of seashore blend with gentle sway
When black as oil the waves reflect the lights upon the bay.

Machines

Earth is full of working machines, and then just see them fly;
Over the land there hovers the work, the art of the human eye.
Metal and rod, piston and gauge, they all inform the whole.
The world is crammed with working machines,
On land, in sea and sky; see them crawl and swim and fly.

Earth is full of working machines, and then just see them dive;
Under the sea a presence lurks, formed by the human mind.
Propeller and blades, engine and gear, they all inform the whole.
The world is crammed with working machines,
On land, in sea and sky; see them roll and drift and dive.

Earth is full of working machines, and then just see them run;
Upon the land beasts are defied, tamed by the human gun.
Muscle and nerve, sinew and claw, they all inform the whole.
The world is crammed with working machines,
On land, in sea and sky; see them rise and fall and die.

Above they are swept by ethereal kind, drifting through in rows;
Upon those shores, the diamond shores, where wanderers repose,
Beauty and grace, bounty of place, they all inform the whole.
It's never crammed, it's never full, its sway beyond compare—
On earth and sea and sky looks down, its presence everywhere.

The Butterfly

A messenger has never been so beautiful, or frail;
Sensing the coming of life, and its end,
Passing on its greeting in the wayward breeze,
And summoning us to sigh and grieve,
In aisles and sunlit passageways.

Alighting where other creatures would be gone,
A tapestry of silk absorbing sun.
But all its stateliness in humble guise,
A costume looking lost in marble halls,
Yet deferential only in its size.

How can we judge the ways it makes us glad?
How many times it strays and makes us sad.
But ever in the summer months, it plays –
Worthy spirit, phantom of the air,
Comforting our pain without a care.

The sun in rhyme

The path to all pleasures leads below; the sea lies deceptively blue,
And without the reins of childhood, liberty unfolds and bursts anew.
A bud has long since blossomed in the salty ground,
The scant rose wavers in its parched cliff top home, and breezes mix the colour, creating sun drenched worlds that blend and flow and quiver;
A face that can't be traced, families once lost and drawn again;
Lightweights bobbing gently in the swell, waving with a frailty
to the sunlit sand and its ancient shell.
Hair is tousled in the ruffling air above, wind impels sensation, expanse defies depiction – imagination too refined to be in rhyme;
A moment savoured but exempt from time

Cromer

A Queen enthrals

How this Queen did smile to every aisle, amid her pleasure, through her pain;
And then enduring to the end, her favour rests upon the pleasure of a man.
From within the brightness of her reign, he is left to contemplate his duty, and his fame.
Treasure matters not to those gone by, but it is tribulation where we stay,
so all the more alluring to behold the constancy of one who held her sway,
at ease with high ambition, little hindered by decay.
Men at arms around her, a sea of gentle faith,
Acquainted with compassion, not untouched by grief.

The ice flow

In the deep Atlantic, poles away, seals are floating, easy prey,
abundant as the life that teems around, pelagic predators at play.
From below, a shifting, bold advance, to shatter every peace, drive out desire, from blood-red hunters who conspire.
Shallow is the ice and deep the sea, and dark green depths of life host killers black and white and free.
Their mission is mere treachery and guile; but they have their beauty.

Swamped by ocean swell and breaking ice, she's gone and lost to sight,
swallowed up by shining bonds in silent brutal strife.
But there is beauty too, not so far away, when mother and her pup play out their mute and sad refrain; lost in the uncaring sea, the cold and bitter main.
Upon the frozen rock of ages they silently reside, regeneration wild,
staring one to another (it seemed an age for them to part),
A look to melt all cold hearts,
Saying their last goodbye,
Surely they had loved,
And surely never die.

Commotion

The buttresses fall, the walls tell wild despair,
The tenement is empty and owners' flocks nowhere;
Around, within, the world has changed:
The hand that wrought commotion admits almighty gains.

New life has passed us by, we sit among the dead;
We hold a share, we cling to it; unease, unfiltered dread.
Our walls are slim, they have some strength, but they may burst apart
when aggravation tears and troubles wear and worry seals the heart.

And once before, the tumult raised far off in distant lands,
Appeared as tongues of flame, a whirlwind in the sand.
Words became the fountain head, a universal rule,
Once spoken then, they tossed and turned, united at their fall.

A settled type of motion now breaks upon the soul, when water flowed
And candles glowed, three names attested here below.
They came to strengthen and foretell the bond approved above,
The dark inheritance of pain now overthrown by love.

Piecemeal

Ragtag but also patient, things will work out fine,
keeping faith with hope and love, it matters not the
time. A fragment of a figure is lost but then a start,
and can be built on to become some monumental art.

But mixture can be questioned, and quality can fade,
a spectacle can once become a small impression made.
To be refined and simple, these two can be the same,
if you can trace a subtle mind and play a steady
game.

Who would have thought to see in place a marvel of a
kind, a living statement of an art, rendered down
from time. Each little flake becomes the mass of
fragments that are gone, till we behold a newer form,
a masterwork in stone.

Vera Lucia

Inured to disappointment, refusing deep regret, the heart that I espied in time, required no epithet. It was just there, a natural touch, reserved and yet refined, the quality of denim girl, an unpretentious mind.

Not so unassuming to live without a fight –
Small, but kindled to a brightness, soft shadow in the eyes.

Dark look of inchoateness, born of tropic climes, yearning for a joyfulness so few of us can find. If only she could dance and sing, a modern pirouette, but there was I a solid frame, my substance and neglect.

And yes I wish I could expand, not retreat to youthful past, or even those more recent bonds, broken, not to last. The early life was sweet and pure but there within they lurk, the seeds of tainted innocence, of pain and dust and doubt.

But I have found a recompense, a lady at her ease, content to witness foolishness with faith and light and truth, treating with sincerity all that we find on earth.

A painting in reverse

Behind a fresco painting, what can there be to find,
nothing but the plaster, nothing but the sand; even
though we excavate, even though we delve, there is
little left more delicate than grit and stones of old.

But what a subtle casing, endowed by graceful mind,
the colours bright as long before, upon the wetted
lime.
We come within the sacred space, encountering its
peace, astonished at the one who crouched, in the
mist of time; colours brushed and running free, living
in a cloud, painted for an age to come, each pigment
for the crowd.

This side of the fresco is all we have to touch, light
was kind within those walls, a canopy above; but
now we have a canvass, to bless the closing day,
within a room, upon the wall, the Lord upon his way.
And so as we consider the depths of yesterday, as we
retire to test the night, to sleep with peaceful dream, a
notion of the past creeps by, behind but deep within.

A village life

What is there about it, a village tinged with green,
some thoughtful flowers in places, some paths by
river streams; an historical encounter, past ancient
homes whose walls, that once were bright with
newness, now crumble as they fall. But that is not the
pattern, most is clean with careful pride; there is work
to keep us well, without and deep inside. We intrude
with glimpse of sitting room, a comforting abode, the
warmth of quiet lighting, and private lives unheard.

The highway often sounding, the railway rolling past,
a village as a passageway, once here but left so fast;
always motion pressing us, but then it too retires, as
day has turned its travail into hardly noticed stars.
Again it breaks the morning on dampened grass and
road, is this some new suburban street attached to
somewhere old? But trees remain, the church is near,
the light is rich and true, and from tidy village
slumber the ancient souls break through.

A City Life Sao Paulo style

Without a true horizon the buildings interfere, and at the very vantage point the open sun appears, to banish what were shadows or make them more severe.

A cultured face in towering size, looks out in coloured squares, a chequered dream in concrete upon the scraper side; a newer image monstrance couched in modern art, there to muse on city streets, below where lovers pass.

She perches on the railing, her floating hair and dress, taken by the altitude, a natural smile impressed. And where the soft wind flourishes the memory restores, such a fleeting glimpse indeed of fragile lives abroad.

On the streets the city is tarnished in my dream, but high above the culture soars and air feels warm and clean.
A trace of dim despondency betrays the mind in this, from fondness of a smile, to semblance of a kiss. But the city is a structure, the city is a gem, a place where no one walks too far when they can dance and run.

And we have travelled miles to taste of family and past, to savour entertainment on the streets – and language flowing fast.
High above the sky is wild, and bare without a cloud, below the ground is sterile, except for vibrant trees, and I am left a foreigner with a mind of mild unease.

Lost Copy

Losing you is simple, finding's hard to trace, once a paper substitute, a living, lost lament, and now a ream of thoughts and tears, unfathomed and unsung, sober treasures sitting there, waiting for their turn, perhaps a little stilted or then a little staid; a floating arch, a canopy of words and hints and thoughts, ideas with their captions playing in a void, as if they're shot by verticals, arising from their grave, but lost in the hereafter without their title page; no knowing what they meant to me, no chance of knowing you, best to be forgotten in the virtual printer queue.

Vindication or the Worm that turned

A perfect explanation of how things came to pass,
cannot be undertaken upon this patch of earth.

Fluid was the journey on which he first began, a boy
without stability, driven who knows where, to
entertain his pleasure amid the mire of youth,
straggling here and pushing there, to follow what was
sent and what was chased, without much thought of
consequence; a flighty innocence.

Steaming through the actions, fast and fleet of step,
walking in directions unknown by hands or feet,
almost thrown about him as he wandered down the
street.

Pierced by cruel derision, knocked and knocking
back, but lacking manly courage to fight off the
attack. It wanted reckless violence it seems from this
remove, but he was good and gentle then, a quiet and
peaceful youth.
But don't destroy the goodness that's sent from up
above, by stolidly refusing to win your own respect,
seeing it as fruitless, and grieving those we love.

Then the journey lengthened and two became as one,
and the life found fabric to share a humble home,
away from youth or childhood and idols we had
known, provided for and guided in a way we never
knew, undecided what to think but sensing what was
true.

And then the phantom journey deep within the mind, where there's little sanctuary and fears and threats abound, placing us in pastures like the stubbled ground, barren, unforgiving, the blind led by the blind.

Such were those once burdened, broken by remorse, those who once were nearly lost, beckoned by recovery but bought at quite a cost.

And then the vindication roars, the dragon eats its words, the ravaging of earth lies still, the guilt once felt now gone; the blame resides within us still but, like revenge, won't stay for long.

Gold windows in the darkness

Gold windows in the upper rooms on the darkened night radiate their life force, like a planet's beams, as a river all in brown gently spreads with stealth, without a seeming current or life to be observed, it's moved by unseen presence, hidden from our sight, without a sound or tremor, escaping into night. Perhaps they watch in brightness, huddled all in one; perhaps they talk together within some dark recess, or pass the lonely evening – in silence.

Inside the old grey farmhouse, above the pockmarked bridge, those lives are imperceptible, who knows the tales untold, shed as in a spectacle of brightly shining gold; reflected light is eerie on the dampness of the road and spreads its spell beyond – behind the river as it flows; inspiring something tuneful within a watching soul, lost within a reverie, standing all alone, singing to a melody of unattended words.

The longest village

It was a day in late summer, cloudy without rain, breezy without bluster, as we strolled hand in hand, impelled and sometimes wistful through the cars on either side, what must have been now coloured by the modern everyday, the highroad and its horses a sepia print of yesterday. We found our way through thresholds, into ancient gloom, showrooms full of antique ware, the softening of carpet upon the creaking stair, glow of things once opulent, creatures under glass, tables, chairs in fashioned oak, volumes sadly languishing in semi-vacant rows.

The spine of the antique village trod in cloud-blown light, was like the sky continuous with byroads at its side; no time to be particular, to find where they may lead, the afternoon is pressing its heart upon our feet. And so the houses cradle, grand and small on either side; but then some lively colour glimpsed, some nature deeply shot, stunning seashore images, at odds with what we've seen; another kind of showroom, escape from old to new, somewhere quaint but magical where light shines bright and true.

So the past and present together they reside, around a lofty village and through each opened door, along a street that stretches far and beckons evermore. Quietened now our pace decays as if on valley floor we follow after rivers, far from wayward cars, an onward stroll becoming now a mix of history, where something lost by gaining ground returns upon the air and draws us close together, in mourning something fair; to stray at last upon a patch of pleasant village green – a sort of destination in a place or in our dreams.

A cenotaph

We are widely summoned to pay that deep respect, we know not how they suffered, their names are with the dead. Not a tomb, but symbol to emphasize the load, the height and depth of feeling – no place of fixed abode.

A host of ready martyrs – for country not for faith – willing for the fight, gone without a trace; but this is sure reminder of all that we have lost, a pillar and a monument to brighten what was dust; a tidy reparation, a line of noble guests, empowered by the spectacle, reddened by the flower, teaching the respectable the residue of power – and showing to the faint heart, the humble and the weak, dead soldiers now grown handsome, the dumb allowed to speak.

The downward depth of life impels us ever on, below the shining stone, reserved for inward calm, the tortured cries of ages mix with gentle throng – of those who take a moment, reflect on all our woes, the sunshine and its shadow a glimmer of our hopes.

But was it once an honour to serve this native land, to quell some distant threat, to right some ancient wrong; against a foe that looked and smelt within a rotten trench, very much the same as us in every grim respect?

Juggernaut

Take me to the eastern shore, that failing piece of
land, where gulls in flight their cries unite with
tempest-bringing rains, and darkness at the midnight
brings its cargo gushing forth, freight upon the docks
and cranes against the sky, fragility that's cast in steel,
those crates with mighty weight.
And from it all the juggernaut, pilot of the road, god
of searing traffic in the chillness of the night,
equipped and fuming principle of power glaring
white.

Pressing still, the land makes way and from the
crumbling coast, the shallow road cuts out a path
through place of no recall, forgotten piece of
wasteland, dredged as if at sea, the dirty place once
pristine, drowned by industry.
Terrain all cast in darkness makes way to city street,
illuminated messenger of never-ending trade, the
watchman and the driver, the goods and their
recourse – with each and every contract they seek to
seal our wealth.

And deep offshore, the passage flows, the wind
pursues forever. Who knows how far the sea will pull,
the aching winds will sever, the little band of driving
men, embattled by the weather.

Stern and serious

Our hardness doesn't flatter, our lack of warmth it tells, and though we're cast as manly the sourness overwhelms. We could be unknown angels or sad but gentle too, instead this face of grit and stone betrays a stricken mind, a little care that's absent, compassion rarely found.

And so this face of ages, the noble and the grand, competes for glory in the round, flattered by an audience, claiming centre ground, but loathing those beneath the wing of their diminished power, depending on the ones despised for praise – becoming blame, when every wrong is manifest – a challenge to their name.

A little kindness does no harm, a blessing passing by, a look dispelling coldness, a smile replacing scorn, a chance to calm a poor heart, forbearance in the storm.

Identity

Aren't we all impassioned, decked in time of war, or wedded to an art of work, ambition to the fore; claimed by competition, pushing at the door, trying to make sense of self in terms of dues and rights, but oftentimes offended and lost without a fight.

An unintended habit, a consequence unfelt, a feeling of obscurity, a never-ending quest, sought but barely questioned a reason for our woes, driven by an impulse to seek we know not what, a happiness that haunts us, but flies and can't be found, stability-identity, a passing peace of mind.

All those we know around us can't make a life entire, but some impeded memory, some underlying past, some reverential feelings allow us then to speak, the words that draw us closer, the love that we receive, within the heart that's close to us, making all complete.

The haunting of what went before

It's like a dream that's gone, unreal walk we had, to village green those years ago, like school so long before, the narrow walls that tower high and then: a bright full day, with dogs that ran or dragged us and troubled those they found, unfettered in their freedom, eating up the ground; but our time then still creeping by, passing one by one those endless chores of nothingness, no aim, no title won.

That field so still, so timeless, the paths still there today, monument to the fallen in trees against the sky, before it was forgotten, now it stretches high; embers of November they gather into fire but what is this remembrance, so dim within my life, just some vague reminders of loss or muffled strife. End the bleak November, call the gentle spring, take the impulse growing, and flight upon the wing.

And so the trail to Robins brook, past the cottage once discrete, now a crowded little plot, a street where all paths meet; but still within those pebbled walls a plaintive cry is heard, the source of some strange wonder, a life increased and shared; the wakened past was uttered and all became as new, a movement on the journey, a joy within a cloud; a village once remote becomes a busy town.

Above and Below

We go to Sabbath blessing, forgive us Lord we pray,
the people close around us, a parish home to stay; we
have some pained reminders of what has gone amiss,
we recall the greatness of what we sense above, and
how we have neglected the little way of love.

But what of those quite unconcerned of little, narrow
ways, of quiet introspection or sounds of ample
praise? They are those whose lives are bent on things
upon the earth, absorbed, obsessed, and taken by all
that's found below, by articles of faith untouched or
unimpressed, seeking single-mindedly another kind
of quest.

And so his message widens, to help us understand, a
different kind of preacher from within a natural land,
a land that needs protecting, in need of fine research,
no small detail unnoticed, to movements in the dark,
and all his generations with science at the heart; a
different kind of creature with a simple kind of hope.

American Candy

Around the usual corner, past the usual shop, traffic now departed and feet upon the prowl, the blackness briefly blasted like electric shock, the doorway widely open, light without a sound, signboard brightly pasted with colours in the night, candy to be tasted, gossip in the news; those paths that have been taken – some are fiction some are truth.

This is a sudden rare sight with a feel of something lost, dark form behind the counter bathed in shedding light, looking for the daybreak, custom once again, needing to run to the early hours, but tethered by boredom and pain.

This is a night for a mystery, the tread of a gumshoe step, the silence of the softness, the chill of the wares inside, the freezers gently shining and the sweets for the morning run; the place is shrouded in darkness, but the untrue light has won.

Salt of the earth

The good is to be tasted, the bad must go to waste but the one who greets a stranger may not at first impress; a kindly kind of gesture, a word without disdain, from one who stands there happy to live a simple life, only seeking fairness within a humble lot, a cheerful undertaking, knowing his way round, at ease with all about him, not sullied by the grime.

This is one who earns his salt, such that can't decay, from dirty occupation he shines as if on fire, a natural entertainer – with enough to pay his way. So to the low and crafty he presents an honest mind, he seems a touch untroubled by dangers he may find, and lets the world go by him while understanding well the trials and tribulations, the worries that befell.

A surgeon slips away

What a noble spirit, what a worthy life, tending to the body, the body of mankind, without a condescension, and lacking disregard, encouraging the humour of those about, around, and using fine attention to cleave an open path, like a story fast unfolding, with a needle in its clasp.

How can he claim his confidence, assurance in his task, to cut the very life of us, shedding blood upon his knife? Years of understanding and born with inner flair, the balance and the artistry and study worth so much, rewarded by the patient, no payment quite enough.

And when the theatre's over, he goes his humble way, seeing in his obstacles a challenge to be met, hoping, surely praying, for healing in his touch and for the years to be as kind as they can ever be – serenity and mildness in his unfailing care, until he's taken from us, slips and drifts away, from a planet needing surgery – more than we can say.

Ideas, events and people

These are things that last, that occupy the mind; the haunting of our places, the rising from the grave, the making of disciples, the lives of holy folk, the women often tender or grieving for their loss – and many times substantial, not just beneath the cross. A tale of high adventure, the products of the hand, the effort of the people, things formed in distant lands.

The temples or cathedrals, the palaces, are planned by dint of understanding the role of everyman. And as they stand impressive when years of war have passed, they remain a monument to every child that's born, each one of whom holds promises to bear for something new – or something old that's built upon to break afresh, anew.

And so events unfolded, churned up by malcontents, the rebels and the foes who fought, the churls with mean intent. The war to end all war is now – but peace is heaven sent. And those who raise the standard on high of all that's sound are those who make these happenings prepare for something grand, like castles for the innocent, raised on holy ground.

And ruling all, the talk we make of these three things that last, is formed by thought and insight, remarks that shadow thought, from gossip to the heights of prose, reflection of the mind, principles that guide us as we move from poor to fine, always pressing onward by the light of inner grace, the force of all this circumstance, ideas taking place.

God speed the plough

Imagine then the oxen, formed for yesterday, pulling for a purpose, slowly making way, harnessed by the ancient yoke, instructed to respond, lumbering steadfastly on their quest to till the ground. And keeping in their company the singing band of folk, a chorus rising gladly, the songs all bright and gay, without a care thereafter, without a thought today.

All is soft and hallowed, all dewy then the day, a heavy scent ascending with birds upon the rise; a call of crows, the sky hangs low, the barns are warm and dry, and without haste the crew resumes with strength and mild refrains, calls of light encouragement, heavy breath and strong, the ox and plough move onward, soft and slow of pace, a day of gentle happiness, a day of inner grace.

Rootedness

We are deeply planted when we find the hallowed ground, a place where we were meant to be, not a shallow grave, rooted in the well of life to seek an atmosphere where all of us can breathe afresh, the deaf allowed to hear, a place without temptation, and one without a care; the life we have can flourish here at least for some short time, till taken up we realise what we have left behind, what every life has sought for, a sweeter taste of death, rooted in the spirit, by every tongue confessed.

Nothing like that

Nothing too fair – things don't go like that
Nothing too fine – but things can be found like that
Nothing too strong – not at the first like that
Nothing too honourable – there's a long wait for that
Nothing too understandable – things slowly transpired like that
Nothing too sensible – often too far from that
Nothing too lasting – seldom it's made like that
Nothing too lean – except for a youth like that
Nothing too bold – times were not ripe for that
Nothing too wild – things were quite tame like that
Nothing too loving – a child had to cry for that
Nothing too esteemed – hidden the virtue of that
Nothing too refined – but things can improve like that
Nothing too equipped – often too late for that
Nothing too respectable – in worldly eyes like that
Nothing too disastrous – but we got near to that
Nothing too sad – there is a break from that
Nothing too painful – not like the worst of that
Nothing too regretful – there must be some of that
Nothing too underhand – no, we were good like that
Nothing too deceitful – we hadn't the head for that
Nothing too healthy – always on the ward for that
Nothing too wise – oh for a taste of that
Nothing too remarkable – but oh quite a tale is that
Nothing too unchangeable – or fixed and set like that
Nothing too lost – we hope and we pray for that

Nothing unread – so much we could have known
Nothing unsaid – more than we can say
Nothing undone – 'the moving finger writes'

Pity the world's a sham – with its ways and means
Pity things are hard – for woman and for man
Pity things don't seem to work out – but they can!

This be some other sort of verse

You fuck them up, your mum and dad.
You may not mean to, but it's done.
You weigh them down with all you have
Then spurn their selfless care and run.

But you were fucked up quite alone,
Dear son you were a trial to bear,
Good friends and neighbours looking on
While you indulged your childhood care

Youth passes on its own mistake,
Man's misery was turned to love;
Remember those who gave life shape
And harmless sleep with them above

This is in response to Philip Larkin, on his own terms, which accounts for the language used.

Just a thought

Lust isn't worth pursuing,
In your head, or in your bed;
You'll only have a good time briefly,
And a long time to repent.
The lust for life is safer, it's honest, robust and right,
As it rears and it rides and it roams, but then rests in the starry night.

Death Doula

He entertains the moment, clothes himself in white, with friends and family looking on, to see him out of life. It is a living funeral, a coffin without depth, he neatly steps into its folds, wrapped in a shroud for death.

He must have tasted somewhere this sense of life undone, the memory and illness unleashed and left to run, images of butterflies, confetti being blown, this is celebration of the bright or dark unknown.

The congregation shuffles into the living space as he himself is settled to contemplate the end, with music gently summoning the spirit of the night, while daytime holds a festival of deep and distant things, the petty and the trivial at flight on tiny wings. And words well up to match the tune, some tales of yesterday, a prayer for the future, contentment for today.

And so it ends and then he's raised from comfy tomb to life, arms outstretched to greet the day, clouds unfurl and guests look on, as harp and organ play.

Meanwhile the dark and subtle Doula, that ancient slave of man, makes a note of earnings, and combs her lustrous hair; a smile for every mourner, 'don't fear, it's not the end' – another date for the diary, next death at half past ten ...

An island in the sky

This could be my last venture, as I wait for the mighty train that blunders on with its baggage, packed to the rim with the wares of life, fettered but somehow free, moving at speed to the distance – will it pause and wait for me?

Or do I stand on my own for the signal to travel the far off land, hoping there isn't much call there, in the virgin state of its ground, for troubles and worries and sadness – destination the last song I found.

It seems like so little before me has passed as a life on its own, summoned now by the future, from a place I've barely known.

Will it always be so lonely, this shore where we pine and die, or will I wake to find unblemished soil, on my island in the sky?

Bright angels in decay

Was there ever once a star that lost its awful shine, a river once dried up that found its source again?

But they were at the pinnacle of life in all its prime, when they refused once more to serve, preferred instead to die.

So yes, it was so possible, if so a vast mistake, that flows now through the ages, the chronicles and pages, the sky that lost its radiance – those dark, once sparkling angels.

At this moment

At this very moment the awfulness appears, when we
are safely sheltered the terrors still unleash their long,
unnerving cruelty, the torture or disease.

We can't escape the clutches of those who wake and
scream, when we are sleeping fitfully, our past a
broken dream. Or even in a crowded place, our
thoughts may turn to war, unrest is seldom far away –
the faces in the street display a sudden nervousness, a
dread of what may be, of what is taking place apart
but close within the mind, removed from every
conscious thought and far from our drab street, but
somewhere there is agony, accompanied by grief.

Peace comes soft and lightly, but doesn't rest for long,
make the most and treasure it, like basking in the sun,
knowing all too well that we won't be at ease until
our unknown strangers can find their source of peace.

A Cowboy's view

A ranger, overcomer, rider seated high, a life above that testifies to the strength of rope and gun, reeling in the steers and bucking every trend, saddled with comfort of leather and living from the land, but fighting for his honour – a hero of a man? Well, he is what dreams are made of, for boys or country men, who follow in the glamour, the rising dust of his fame, the horseshoes clapping loudly, the sun beating down with acclaim.

Riding like a madman, caught in a wind of rage, battling to tame a thrusting mount, lost in a fury of speed and sweat, spurs piercing the tenderness and blood as an emblem shed. But he is just a poor man, a loner of a kind, yearning to find a posse of men, a crowd or a rodeo, the thrill of a creature broken, a brand that he can own. Always searching, scouring the land, ever on the run, but loved by the simple maiden, and the women he's looked upon.

A Tyrant's view

Inclement weather of a febrile mind, storms and seasons fly in his eyes; then placid and childlike he smiles and he plans, fond of his armies but scared of the deep, shut in an enclave while rampant in sleep, beaming with conquest but bound up with fear – a primitive battle too much of a threat, as he quietly retires to be used in his head.

Tackled and beaten by the one who employs the worst of a nation – destroyer of joys. Then the fleets and the fancies roll as if drunk , and the distant drum that unsettles the world calms like a heartbeat his lost raging words.

As if there's no tomorrow

There will be no regrets, no consequence to bear, if we just live today entire and leave the field to chance, unworried by the rising sun, or the setting that never lasts. Tomorrow is the enemy, it must be conquered now, and every vexing memory is simply lost or found, those sordid little efforts to rob our peace of mind.

So never onward seek to stray, for all before us lengthens, here and now for once and all we resolve the present, and trampling on the pristine ground of each new fresh today, we fight or revel gloriously, and never feel decay. How to shun the happy day with not a remnant left, when we enjoy without a judge the spoils of innocence, the pleasures of a life unspent, without inheritance?

All in private

The hollow houses plant foursquare their imprint on the street, a fading sun of winter lights the untouched rooms, and every conversation stalls or armchair chatter fails, while trees without a single leaf, or just a tender stem, unveil the deep discomfort of those who hunker down, banished for the season, quiet or enthralled by vapid entertainment, by sadness passing by, or tales without an ending, bleakness in the mind – we are somewhere ghostly, we're closely undefined.

Then, of all, I saw her once, out walking with the dog, a little thing in tatters, pulling at its cord, and later on retreating to places they have known, a boon perhaps of comfort, a mystery of a room, where a figure ladylike may dream of sunny days, her style a little haughty, her eyes averting gaze.

These are strange companions, seen but never known, closeness is no company when walls their compass draws, throwing darkened shadows within and on the road; they are faint reminders that somebody is there, but no one in particular, a story never shared.

Born and bred

Yes there was a place somewhere, beyond the scope of time, or any probability, unlit and undisclosed, not even chance describes it, fate gets somewhere close. And there we rested for a day, in the arms of love, until a greater urgency called us from above; within the bearing and the breeding an inner life was planned and long before our making our ending was discerned.

But how have we arrived at this, to reach and share our goal, a family emerging by little awkward steps to guide us or to fail us, to share and bear our loss, sometimes uneventful, at times to reassure, and often full with meaning, its value more and more? Yes there was a place somewhere, and we have fed the ground; it was before so barren, but now a fertile grave we've found.

If I could write a sonnet

If I could write a sonnet, poor reflection of the Bard, something more effusive with some authentic charm, loosening and freeing words, words I've hardly known, rhyming in the depth of sense subtle fours and twos, and finding in the love of verse a lover's pleasing muse. Then I would form a song for us, one for every age, attuned to all who listen, a gift for all who speak, music of the minstrels and epics of our speech.

If I could write a sonnet, and raise it as a prayer and cast it to the elements, to spread its message wide and capture with its innocence some measure of the mind, then I would be a lesser type of those who went before, for they would play with syllables and craft a proper line, imagination flying wild but held with gentle sway, like images upon a shelf or corals in the sea, shedding words of beauty for the sense of you and me.

Wollemi

They are truly ancient, perhaps a fossil once, keep your eyes wide open, widely on the watch, for they were found when once thought dead, in fissures in the land; the far away Blue Mountains be our natural guide as we interpret ages gone, the wild where fern-like grow, the trees of the Wollemi pine a dinosaur might know.

And their jagged greenness, their upward soaring height, those leaves so svelte and new, turning then to clusters, shining with the dew of early tropic mornings, awake for years now past, sheltered in the canyon grove, lost treasure in the Park.

They looked on when I once sought the harmony of trees, an arboretum sharing land with those of many hues, from many climes and continents, now placed with care to grow and reach for England's southern skies, so far from land they know.

But they seem richly satisfied with their new fostered home and I am now enamoured to find them where I tread, their mystery, their elegance, a new world taste of wine, like a rose placed with an orchid, so different yet sublime..

Nearly understood

Can we see the fullness of a truth or saying said?
Perhaps the gist of finer things or sense of something
read, subtlety elusive, thought that's second best? But
with a simple living stroke, the brush or pen can
speak, and what was cloaked in darkness can walk
into the light, the heart unveiled uncovering the
ruggedness of art.

For in its wake equations and finely-tuned excess
seem gentle with a decency, with rationale expressed,
but riddled with the artifice of giving us the lie that
they can be all things to us and can at last outlive the
thought of being human, transcend the great abyss
between the seeing and the knowing – and where's
the God in this?

Alma mater

All defining mothers, known or not so well, perhaps a total stranger, but love can bind them all. They controlled our heartbeat, but now we're spread abroad, we're sent to find another soul, a partner for our lives, not the one of flesh and blood but one that fosters care, a place we've known from when still young, a regimen to heal, or help us grow and flourish, recover and reveal.

And this old place, not meant for all, a start of things to be, call it education, call it chemistry, a teacher who was kind to us, who tried to understand the pains of every woman, the making of a man.

And nowhere else could play its part for it creates and grows into a life that's moulded by this and that about; better paths there could have been and better lives no doubt, but we were simply nourished, a romance from the start.

A stony sort of pathway, for some engulfed in pain, a lifetime of renewal, untaught, untutored road, whatever on the journey, the past is always heard. And looking back we always yearn for learning more profound, for dignity and promise, respect from all around.

We languish with nostalgia and all that could have been, holding on to visions of all those dreaming spires, seeing rainbows fondly from the windows of the mind – and in a sense it deeply matters, we're fostered then we die.

Encounter (Candlemas)

He was once presented, from a towering sky above, to an old man in the temple who saw the light and knew that all he had been promised and all he dared to hope was bound up in that image, the source of all that's true.

It was the tribe of ages blending, in the dark and soulful place, with those who wait expectant for a light on which to gaze, the glory of a nation, already purified – by a mother and her baby, encountered and espied.

The candle flames still flicker and move from hand to hand, in whose feeble clutches the light will ever burn, keeping pale reminder of the soaring star above, and a cry heard in the heavens, like a sudden spear of love.

Man's empty praise

If all the praise we're offered is like some flattery, a medal for a talent, dubious at that, a supply of adulation for what we haven't got, then all the world's aflutter with all the silly charm of winning and sensation, the strength of those who run, the sweat of those who fight, endearing to the public with famed awards in sight.

Consider every loser who struggles here below, or those who build the monuments, the temples of a kind; their sweat is that of dying, their place of resting never found.

A testament to decadence is lauded all around, the theatre of the senses, an ecstasy on high that erupts from every triumph, applause for those who shine. While the shock of all that plenty, the stubbornness of greed, demotes all those who can't defy the madness of a crowd, the spectacle of greatness, the victor's mighty cry – echoed by a people, but not assented to on high!

Absurdity

I'm angry with brutality and weapons piling high,
seen as an investment in future children's lives, we
must have more protection, so keep them piling high.

This is what we're offered to keep the wolf at bay,
mighty reinforcements, tanks to be destroyed,
warships that have floundered, lives in disarray.

But the wolf is still at large, St Francis tame him now,
for all the weapons in the world won't rid us of the
beast, the one that prowls within the mind and rids
the soul of peace.

The little men with bitterness, hostile to all kind, the
stronger men with anger, fighting in the depths, the
women holding dead ones, the children torn to shreds
and all the while the newsbeat, proclaiming this or
that, absurdity turned normal with funds on every
side, flooding through the tunnels, a never ending
tide.

We might as well increase our load, and pour it on the
fire and see the whole world pass away, at least we'd
fight no more.

Heedlessness

Take it as a warning, a piece of sound advice, or carry on regardless and launch into the new, a project or proposal, swept along apace, with novelty the benchmark, one without a test, the ending in the deepness of water or of space.

Prepare the little children, dressed in white for best, trailing through the endless passageways of faith, constrained by narrow corridors of working to the law – will they heed the message as they approach their choice, will they grow in stature, march from dark to light, or go their own way blithely with a precipice in sight?

And when the greyness calls us, losing strength and peace, will we quite surrender the things of yesterday, graciously enduring the loss of all our gains, our strength retiring gently to rest like babes again – or will we rage like ranting ones, long into the night, and reach too far for bursting stars, falling from the heights?

Reverting to type

In those distant days of dust and wilderness, utterance of joy began to change what had once become and left us free but senseless, blank page for writing on.

Within the sacred sycamore and seated in it bows we sought a new approval to mend our former ways, and in its arms we feasted until the eve of day upon the flow of movement below where he would walk, the offer of a new dawn, the words to alter minds, as we sat ungainly within the tree of life.

It is sure and shapely, this tree now unadorned, and we can grow in stature, to change and be transformed, sitting there, uplifted, but we must watch and hope – for someone fells the symbol and spoils the virgin earth, and we are left forsaken and lost without the light of shining ones and promises, as man reverts to type.

Transformation

We need to be transformed, be created once again, to usher in the bright day, with trumpet sound and harp, when shackles are discarded and suffering is past. For all the entertainment and promises of youth have left us poor and needy still, grasping for the truth.

The new day is upon us now, but we are cloaked in fear, and darkness has the dominance, when light should reappear.

May the old world crumble, through steadiness of heart, to build upon our littleness, the health we once enjoyed, the spoken word to reassure, the charity we seek; to find at last the remedy, that place of perfect ease.

Solitary swansong

It was indeed a winter's tale, the river lost to sight, what could be seen beneath the bridge was metal brimming light; not the light of moon or stars, but from the empty street above.

And where I stood in mistiness beside the shiny lane, there too a silent swan appeared, statuesque in frame. Head stretched back within its wing, all appeared to sleep; a one-eyed apparition – motionless at midnight – white and bleak.

We stood and stared a little while, unsensed without a sound, the air was damp and desolate, significance unbound. And then a song, a muted hush, stirred among the leaves and every swan that ever was joined transparently in the death of beauty, the vacant sound of peace.

I made a move to break this spell (to leave seemed so unfit), and as I turned a cat had come, so curious to greet. On a spin it turned and ran, for safety down the path, and I was left to wander on, a shadow of my past.

Milton Keynes UK
Ingram Content Group UK Ltd.
UKHW020353240824
447344UK00004B/296

9 781789 634754